Local Marketing in a Digital World

By Robert Dickson

Disclaimer and Copyright Notification:

The ideas in this book come from the author's personal experience and research. Your results may vary according to a wide variety of circumstances, not the least of which being the effort you put into applying the concepts you're about to learn.

While I make every effort to ensure that I accurately represent all products and services, there can be no guarantee that your results will match examples published in this report.

In the case of web links included, please note that the author and distributor can't be responsible for content not of their creation.

About the Author

Robert Dickson began his Internet Marketing career in 2002, building affiliate websites. He started a local website design and development business in 2008. After tons of research, and much trial and error, he has determined the best ways to promote locally-based small businesses online.

Robert's Website Services Firm, **LocalMarketingWeb.com** has helped dozens of local businesses improve their websites, and gain more clients.

Why Online Marketing?

The Internet was designed by the government, and in its infancy was used for library catalogs and the exchange of information between braniacs in and out of the academy.

In the late 1990s, it became splashier, a nice counterpart to traditional media: we began reading magazines and newspapers on our desktop computers. And large companies began to sell and advertise their products online.

However, as we all know, there is no longer a culture of information control in which a small elite has access to our eyes and ears via the Internet. It is no longer used for particular types of information by types of people, but for everything, by everyone.

Because people can quickly -- almost magically -- punch some buttons and find a car wash in Oklahoma City or read reviews of physical therapists throughout New England, businesses in turn are in possession of great power. It is now easy and affordable (with basic services usually free) to put your product in the World's lap. The hardest thing is keeping up with what's available and with strategies for putting these tools best use.

Thisbook will teach you ways to not only reach new customers, but to get your existing customers to spend more money with you, and do it more often!

The Explosion of Online Searching

Digital Business analyst comScore reports that Google served up 10.7 billion searches in April, 2011. A year later, that monthly total was 11.4 billion. Many Google searches are for medical information, facts for homework, or other "research" purposes. However, we know that online shopping and searching for information on products has been on the rise in recent years. And while big corporations and online-only establishments like Amazon.com were early heavy-hitters in e-commerce, it is becoming increasingly common for people to use the Internet to scope out local businesses.

Google reports that 20% of all searches are local. That amounts to 2.28 billion local searches in April, 2012. The U.S. Census Bureau's Statistical Abstract of the United States (May, 2011) reports that 71% of adult internet users and 55% of all adults buy products online; the search engine Milo tells us that 42% of shoppers responding to a survey check a store's inventory online before going to the physical stores. 47% reported using their smartphone to find local information, including shopping information. 60% reported having researched products several times per month with a mobile device.

To demonstrate the upward swing of this trend, another survey finding was that 40% of respondents said they research products online more now than a year before.

This research can involve using search engines such as Google, but can also—as we'll discuss at length later— involve using social media. In other words, going to a business's Facebook page can be an effective form of research for a customer, that is if that business is proactive about providing information.

However, using social media can involve more than just looking at information provided by the business. Paul Marsden, writing for socialcommercetoday.com, says, "we use social media to research options—from the shared ratings and reviews of strangers, to being open to the ideas, endorsements and behaviour of people we know and trust."

Having introduced this new world, one of integrating web browsers with the stores on the streets in our town, let's take a step back and form a nice contrast between this sort of business-customer relationship and one from the past: the Yellow Pages. Traditionally, the Yellow Pages had been the "go to" source for local businesses. What business wasn't listed there?

But with the transition to Internet-based local search, potential customers are becoming less and less likely to use the Yellow Pages, and not only because of the convenience and speed of the internet. They're also looking, to quote from Marsden, to "research options" in the form of reliable reviews and other information about the companies they're considering – something that simply isn't possible with print advertising.

The Yellow Pages Dilemma

Several years ago, Yellow Pages providers realized that they need to do something to keep from becoming extinct. One of the solutions they've attempted is internet-based Yellow Page directories.

These directories work much like the printed version. Your ad gets placed in the appropriate category, on the assumption that people will use those directories to find local businesses. But in reality, these types of sites get very little traffic - Google, Bing and Yahoo are the places that people turn to when they're looking for local businesses:

Therefore, creating content to be indexed by search engines is a much more attractive option. It allows for these advantages:

- greater flexibility in the presentation of your business

- lower costs, particularly if we consider large ads in the Yellow Pages.

- the ability to update or refine to your ads as often as you want. Compare that to a print ad that can only be changed annually.

And if we compare an online presence to Yellow Pages print directories, the difference is more dramatic. According to a study that the Department of Health and Human Services at the National Center for Health Statistics ran from January to June, 2010, approximately 24.9% of all adults live in households with only wireless phones, which means they may not receive a Yellow Pages directory.

That means nearly 25% of your target market may be leaving you behind for the quicker, sleeker Internet.

And interestingly, even more children (29%) live in households with no landline phone. So as those children become adults and move out on their own, these numbers are expected to grow.

Connecting With Your Customers

Carefully considering your online presence and being sure to make it as large as possible is crucial. The ease with which online searchers can find information creates a paradox. It may be easy for them to find *you,* but it's also easy for them to find your competitors. Therefore, the peril in not having a large online presence, in not coming up in a Facebook search for a particular business, not having sponsored ads or being listed in Google Places, is great. Wherever your users may look, it's a good idea to be there. Conceptually, it's a matter of meeting your customers where they are.

First off, you'll need to be sure you're coming up high in the results pages for the Big Three search engines: Google, Yahoo and Bing. Of the three, Google gets the largest percentage of searches (66% in April 2012, according to comScore) so it is the first place you should focus your efforts.

There are several aspects to having a presence in Google:

- The organic search results

- Sponsored ads

- Google Places

- Google Images

- Google News

- Google Video

All components of Google, these are independent of each other. We're going to cover them all in detail in this book, but it's important to remember that each of them works separately from the others so you want to loom large in as many as possible. Appearing in most or all of them will create a strong impression with your customers, and make them much more likely to choose you over another business.

I like to call this the Perpetuation of Success. In the old days, which companies were seen on television and in magazine ads? Only the ones who could afford these ads— the most successful. The presence of the slick ads themselves gave off an aura—and denoted—success.

Today, many people will carry over that way of thinking, and perceive a business with a large online presence to be worthy of that presence. They may think that more successful businesses show up higher in search results or that they are able to hire a PR staff.

So, if you make yourself your own PR engine and aggressively market yourself, the impression of success you create will perpetuate itself, bringing in more and more dollars and more and more opportunities.

So let's look at some ways to set up this aura of success, beginning with the various Google components. We're going to focus on Google in most because it is the most hit, but virtually everything we cover translates to Bing and Yahoo as well.

Google+ Local

Formerly known as Google Places, Google+ Local is a component of Google that creates Places Pages for businesses. Google search results contain a Places component, high in the overall results. If you search for, say "record store," Google reaches into cyberspace, plucks your IP address to determine your location, and gives you results in your area. If you type in a location for which you'd like to find these record stores, say, Boston, the results will override your location and give you the location you want:

Map for **record store Boston**

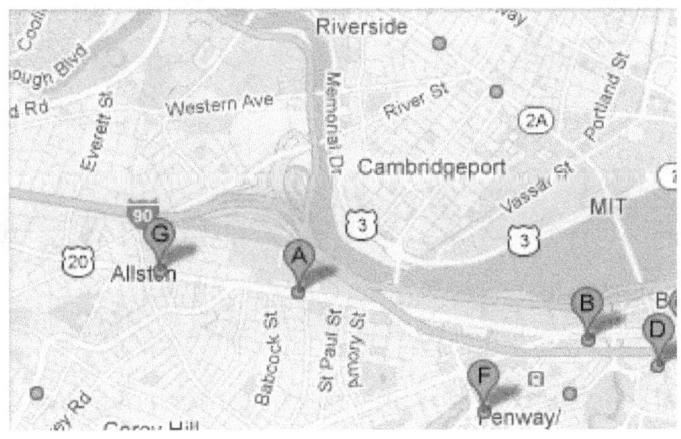

This map is on the right of the results page, and one can see that a business that has set up a Google Places account, which causes it to be shown here, is going to have a clear advantage over one that hasn't. Next to this map, in the center of the results page, is a listing for each business:

In Your Ear!
www.iye.com/
5 Google reviews
↳ Rhode Island Store - Contact Us - About Us

(A) 957 Commonwealth Avenue
Boston
(617) 787-9755

Nuggets
www.nuggetsrecords.com/
4 Google reviews

(B) 486 Commonwealth Avenue
Boston
(617) 536-0679

Newbury Comics
www.newburycomics.com/
Score: 23 / 30 - 26 Google reviews

(C) 332 Newbury Street
Boston
(617) 236-4930

Looney Tunes
plus.google.com
2 Google reviews

(D) 1106 Boylston Street
Boston
(617) 247-2238

Barnes & Noble
store-locator.barnesandnoble.com/store/2115
Score: 20 / 30 - 12 Google reviews

(E) 800 Boylston Street
Suite 179
Boston
(617) 247-6959

Note that under each store is a link to customer reviews of each, a subject we'll explore in a minute. The main point here is that a Google Places listing guarantees you a distinctive, eye-catching place near the top of Google search results.

Get your business found on Google

An account is free, though it does require a Google account (also free). In addition to being listed in results, your business will get a Places Page, on which you'll list your basic information. But, better, you'll have a chance to offer coupons and other detailed product information, as well as posting photos and videos.

One feature of Google Places you may wish to take advantage of—at the time of this writing also free—is the business photo shoot. You've seen slightly dark, unflattering photos of businesses, those taken by the owner himself. The business photo shoot will allow you, if you're in a select area, to have a photo taken by a trusted photographer arranged by Google. Here's a shot of the restaurant Spice Market in New York City:

Spice Market, photo from Google

Not only is it of professional quality, but it is part of a panoramic shot of the restaurant—the user can drag her mouse to view a 360° picture of your establishment. It just takes your enthusiasm and effort to enhance the marketing of your business.

A testimonial posted on Google's Business Photos page, from Sara Creighton, owner of Washington Square Park Dental, explains that as a result of using this services, "We have friends, who have never seen our office, express how impressed they are with the space."

Customer Reviews

Roger Ebert is an international celebrity, having been a guest on major talk shows, and having sold millions of books. He isn't a director, actor, or even a stunt man. He has no part in the creation of movies—his relationship to them is reviewing them, helping us decide which movies to see, and indeed helping us establish criteria for evaluating movies. The fact that his skill in this area has made him just as recognizable as Steven Spielberg, Scarlett Johansson, or Zoe Bell shows the premium our culture places on the opinions of others.

However, the information environment of today is so hyper-democratic that it includes and has made a place for the observations of millions of armchair Roger Eberts. Goodreads.com and Scrid.com are two websites devoted mostly to everyday people sharing opinions about books; there are thousands of analogous websites for just about every product imaginable; there are companies whose product is templates for businesses to use to get customer feedback.

To refer to the Ease Paradox, above, it is easy for people to write reviews. It is likely, then, for your competitors to have reviews of their products. A consumer is going to favour a description over a void, so having a mechanism for feedback is key. Google Places provides the infrastructure for customer feedback, and web marketing experts recommend finding a way to encourage your customers to post reviews.

Clearly, you would do this when you can see a customer is happy. To the extent that you can control it, you of course want positive reviews. We'll discuss handling negative reviews in a few pages. But one point to make now is that negative reviews aren't always damaging to your business and shouldn't necessarily be feared.

There are two main reasons for this.

- *Reviews are descriptive*—imagine your friend says, "don't go that deli, their sandwiches are all bread with not enough meat." Obviously, you *will* go to that deli if you're a bread lover.

- *Rants are not convincing*—I recently saw a review of a motel that whined about how long it took the person at the front desk and about the limited selection in the free breakfast. It gave me more information about the negativity of the person writing it than negative information about the motel. I needed a place to stay on a trip, and chose this motel mostly because of the price. Now, I may be a stickler for fast service and a big (free) breakfast, but reading this review, I didn't feel I could trust this huffy reviewer. How long is a long time to wait? How little cereal and toast is too little? What he described seemed like every complimentary breakfast I've seen in a moderately-priced motel. Since this reviewer seemed like a chronic complainer, I didn't feel I'd have the same petty complaints if my experience were the same as his.

In both of these scenarios, I have found out *something* about these businesses, and I can use my own judgment. As a business owner, you won't be thrilled if you get complaints like the one about the motel, above, but hopefully a rant that seems as though it was written by an arch enemy will be balanced by more reasoned ones.

In any event, an absence of reviews creates the impression no one is using your business and doesn't do anything to make it stand apart from other words on a crowded computer screen.

In general, the principle of Completeness is key. If your places Page (or an analogous service you may choose) is full of pictures and videos, not only does this give useful information to potential customers, but it helps you exude enthusiasm and professionalism. Next to your business with its panoramic photos, videos describing services, pictures of smiling staff and happy customers, and feedback with comments, won't businesses without these features seem to have their head in the sand?

As mentioned, the Internet absolutely crawls with customer reviews, so a presence in Google Places is just one avenue for reviews.

Review Sites

Another place that it's important to maintain an active presence is review sites, including:

- Yelp.com
- Where.com
- Citysearch.com
- Insiderpages.com
- Yahoo Local
- Google Maps

These sites are local business directories that also allow people to post reviews. Much like any other website we've discussed, you need to maintain a presence here if you want to be able to manage your brand and what people are saying about it.

Yelp.com has been around since 2005, and Google Analytics reports the site had a monthly average of 71 million unique visitors in the first quarter of 2012. Its unique niche is that it rewards reviewers—it has Elite badges to dole out to acknowledge their "well-written reviews, a fleshed-out personal profile, an active voting and complimenting record, and playing nice with others." In other words, the site makes a concerted effort to reward thoughtful, balanced reviews, as opposed to rants. It reports that in the first quarter of 2012, more reviews gave the maximum 5 stars than any others, 37%, with 12% giving one star.

As with Google Places, a business can set up an account on yelp rather than just letting a reviewer come along and mention your business. You can then publically comment on user reviews—getting in the discussion to "manage your brand" is a topic we'll give its due attention later.

Citysearch.com was referred to as "the leader" in review sites in a 2008 article by Saul Hansell of *The New York Times,* and has been around since the late 90's, during which time many other review sites came and went.

Managing Your Brand

Again, the importance of having an account with these sites, or at least monitoring the reviews, is not only to find areas for improvement or keep tabs on what people are saying, but also to become part of the conversation.

Negative reviews, while open to interpretation, and as I argued above, not always a death knell, can clearly be dangerous. One reason for this is that they could appear high in the search results for your business, creating a searcher's first impression of you. Some readers will carefully evaluate comments they read, and some will not.

And a review that doesn't characterize the writer as a chronic complainer could still contain inaccurate information, perhaps the result of an honest misunderstanding.

The solution is to be part of the discussion. As mentioned above, Google Places, yelp.com, and other review sites allow for businesses to respond to comments. (Later we'll discuss "standard" social networking sites like facebook and twitter that will also provide opportunities to address problems customers may express with your business.)

Let's go back to the example of a rant about a motel. Let's change the scenario so that the customer has a legitimate complaint. Say he writes a review on one of the review sites listed above and says he requested a wakeup call during his stay "last Thursday," and didn't get one, which caused him to be late to his job interview.

One option as a business owner would be for you to apologize for the mix-up, taking the customer's word for it. Using the date of the review and going back to the previous Thursday, perhaps you remember an issue or emergency that took your attention from a wakeup call. If you are so moved, you could ask the reader to contact you to try to work out a solution, such as a partial refund or a coupon for a future stay. This characterizes you as

- professional and thorough—a business owner who cares enough to read reviews by the average person

- reasonable and fair—not only did you not try the easy way out of calling this person a liar, but you took responsibility. You've made the mistake seem like what it was, the kind of forgivable mistake made by any business.

Consider who this will compare you to your competitor who isn't even aware of what is written about his business.

In the case of something you find factually inaccurate—say, a customer claiming he was overcharged when your records show otherwise—it will be your word against his. In some cases, damaging, seemingly unfair claims about your business will be an ugly side-effect of the hyper-connected world we now live in. But not only should this be offset by the many benefits of free marketing via the Internet, but you also have the ability to address these issues.

As mentioned above, many people respond well to someone who comes across as mature, reasonable, and fair. Therefore, calmly stating that there's been a misunderstanding and that your records contradict the reviewer's claim will at least give readers your side of things, so they can make up their mind.

Some Guidelines for Responding to Negative Reviews

- Choose your battles – let common sense and good judgment be your guide in recognizing comments that just don't need a response. Be sure not to come off as the Comments Cops, which will make you look argumentative and possibly defensive. The best comments to address are those for which you have clear, convincing information to the contrary, or that allow you to address a reader's concerns.

- Take the high road – don't rise to the bait of childish comments or any other malicious behaviour that will arise. Thank the author for her ideas and suggestions, and mostly, for her business. Orient things toward moving forward positively, and gently point out the positive reviews you will probably receive.

Social Media

Having discussed some concepts having to do with managing your brand by keeping up with comments floating around, we now dovetail into the related issue of maintaining a presence on Social Media sites such as Facebook and Twitter.

These tools give you other, very effective ways to customize the way in which you stay closely connected to your customers.

Having a Facebook page is becoming more and more important, because people have come to expect it. There are over 600 million users on Facebook, and if you don't have a presence there you're missing out on a lot of potential business.

Facebook creator Mark Zuckerburg is on record as saying—on more than one occasion—that he wants Facebook to essentially *be* the Internet. He wants users to view youtube videos, find recipes and other analogous information, play games, and listen to music all without leaving Facebook. There's no doubt that the information shared by our friends on Facebook will never satisfy all of our needs, replacing all other activities we do online. However, with people spending some increased amount of time on Facebook, it's clearly important to have a presence there.

Facebook started out as a way to connect on a personal level, and that's precisely how businesses can use it to market locally. Having "friends" of your business page who you may know personally, with whom you've done business in the past, who play in your volleyball league or go to your church can help make you feel comfortable relating in a friendly manner. This will give new "friends" a friendly impression of your business, and make them feel like part of a community.

There's no question that you are in business to sell your product, and that time spent on marketing is there to do just that. Therefore, it's hard to blame someone who concludes that a Facebook account for, say, Julie's Candy Shoppe, is there only to post information of Valentine's Day sales or other discount items. Julie may post every so often just to pitch a few products or to essentially remind people of her shop on Spruce Street.

It makes sense, but research and experience has shown this will have limited effects. People do not log in to Facebook to view ads or to be sold something. Ultimately, the key factor is psychological, and the psychological need here is the old and common need for people to connect. It's important to spend your time (which, we are told, is money) wisely. Orient it toward forging connections with your audience. This is means having a *social strategy* and not just a marketing strategy.

The first step to developing a good Facebook presence that utilizes a social strategy is, of course, generating a good batch of "friends" or people who "like" your page. These people will see what you post in their news feed, and may choose to visit your page to see what you've posted. Naturally, one way to do this is to make friends requests of your personal friends, hoping to branch out to their friends, and with people from local businesses and organizations who show interests relating to your business. Of course, giving thumbs up and commenting on posts from other local businesses (and individuals) can make people want to reciprocate, or at least click on your avatar and visit your page.

<u>Creative Posting</u>

The social strategy, trying to form and be part of a community, will require you to think creatively. We already know it's free, and it needn't take a lot of time either. Remember, it's about using time *well*, not necessary using a lot of it. As far as text-based posts or links, here are some ideas

- Valuable news and information- Julie, our candy shop owner, could post recipes. These could either be sweet-tooth items, (possibly incorporate items she sells), or entrees. After you've had your chicken marsala, you need a dessert, right?

- Community-oriented post – Julie can earn good will by posting a link to information on a local church's food drive or an organization's fundraiser. It could be the play staged by the local high school. Maybe her neighbor's daughter is in the play, which means Julie is acting more as a *person* than as a business owner. Don't think people won't notice that.

- Open-ended questions or polls – The communication doesn't have to be one way, with you playing the role of old-school media, a newspaper or television station. Give your users a voice. Ask them their favorite doughnut filling or favorite downtown bar to frequent.

All of these communications do something very important, which is to show Julie's friends she is interested in doing more than bombard them with sales pitches. Certainly, when someone comes in to her shop, she has time to chat with them about the high school's play or a recipe the customer saw in a magazine. Why can't Facebook be an extension of this?

In the case of useful information, whether it be recipes, articles about desserts, hosting birthday parties, news articles relevant to the community (having no tie in to Julie's business, per se), it serves to give value to your page. It gives people a reason to pay attention to what you post, rather than skimming past it. And when it is time for you to advertise your sales, these will seem like other helpful information you post.

Now, let's discuss creative uses for posting photos. In addition to very useful photos of tempting tortes and peanut-butter cups, Julie can:

- Feature an employee of the month with a photo and a brief profile

- Show photos, if available, of the candy being made

- Take and share photos of customers, who may be familiar to many of the "friends" of her page

- Share photos of the walk for cancer Julie and one of her employees participated in last weekend

- Share photos of the Small Confectioner's Conference in San Diego

- Re-post (in Facebook terminology, this would be to "share" whereas, above I've used the word in its normal sense) photos of the middle school's basketball championship game originally posted by Dale, who owns the photocopy business down the street. *Amy's Candy Shop Congratulates Our Jaguars!*

Finally, there are videos.

- A video greeting. This can be Julie recording text played over still photos of various candies and/or the interior and exterior of her shop.

- A monthly look at a new or featured product

- A video of how particular pieces of candy she sells are made

- Clips of food shows featuring Rachel Ray or Emeril, or from cooking competition shows

As with the other content, above, part of the idea is to connect to people. If someone in her area loves Emeril but missed that episode, he may be happy to see it posted. He'll comment on it, and Julie will comment back. At some point, perhaps as he drives past Julie's shop on the way to Mega Groceries, he thinks, "hey, I should stop in and say hi to her and get a few treats for the kids. It's important to support small businesses."

So, we've seen what the social strategy is all about, and how it can allow you to engage in customers in a way that is appealing to them. Now, you may be saying that it's not your job to congratulate the local softball team or to post miscellaneous videos. As with everything in this book, you do have to use the advice in a way that suits your style and is comfortable for you. But it's important to keep in mind a couple of things. First, the world is changing and has changed, and communication is now becoming everyone's job. And while it may seem corny at first, the results you'll receive from more creative posts will make it worth it, and you may find it well within your comfort zone before long. As for the time it takes, remember that re-posting something you receive in *your* Facebook news feed takes less than half a second, while getting something from the web can take maybe the full second if the website in question offers a "share on Facebook" widget.

Furthermore, while these sorts of posts may sound like they would significantly add to your workload, if you consider spending a few seconds approximately once a week, it's not an appreciable amount of time. Not only would you not need to make more than a few posts a week, the vast majority of all tips on social networking strongly encourage you *not* to do so. It isn't necessarily advantageous to post a lot of content. Don't allow your customers to feel bombarded or to get sick of you. The idea is to spend a small amount of time making highly effective posts that should create wonderful ripple effects.

Twitter

Twitter was launched in the Summer of 2006 and is now consistently among the 10 most-visited websites. It is, of course, organized around "tweets," short up days of no more than 140 characters. It can be useful for sending out messages about special offers and other news, but more importantly it's another way for your customers and potential customers to contact you, since it's possible to send messages via Twitter.

Twitter is often used as a companion to Facebook, with people tweeting a link to a Facebook post. Items you post on Facebook can easily become buried in your friends' news feeds, pushed down below the first page of most recent feeds, so using Twitter to point these posts out can be important.

Pinterest

Readers of *Newsweek* or *TIME* are familiar with the new, much-hyped, and rapidly-growing social networking site Pinterest.

Pinterest is a site for sharing photos and other information by "pinning" an item from the web (or from your hard drive) to a "board" for a particular category. It is visually-oriented, and quickly got a reputation as a place for brides-to-be to find gowns and other pieces of the wedding puzzle, or for people to share recipes view eye-catching pictures. However, you can link to articles, homepages, anything represented by a picture. While at the time of this writing, the site is just shedding its image as being for women or those interested in interior design and recipes, it figures to be adopted by just about everyone before long. It broke the record for fastest time reaching 10 million unique U.S. monthly visitors, and has caught the attention of people in the web marketing business.

The site can be of use for any business, but may be of best use for those with a very visual line of products such as furniture, food, and clothing. You create boards, which you give titles such as "men's casual wear," "women's shoes," etc. and organize your photos accordingly. To some extent you can think of a pinboard as an equivalent to a photo album in Facebook.

Like any other social media, Pinterest allows people to group together—you can "follow" a particular board or all boards created by a particular user. When you log in, you will see the most recent pins on any of these boards, and your followers will see yours.

Here are the boards, for various types of furniture, for the Australian Furniture company, Fantastic Furniture:

A customer whose eye is caught by and who clicks on the main image for one of these boards goes into the board, where she can click on a particular item:

Mobile Marketing

Mobile marketing—reaching your customers through their smartphones and other devices--is a huge growth opportunity for local businesses. A 2012 Internet Trends report by Mary Meeker of venture capital firm Kleiner, Perkins, Caulfield & Byers reports there are now 1.1 billion 3G mobile subscribers, a number increasing 37% per year.

The lastest edition (Mar. 2012) of a joint study by Pew Research Center's Internet & American Life Project and Elon University's Imagining the Internet Center advises us that 10 billion mobile Internet devices will be used by 2016.

However, not enough businesses approach mobile marketing correctly.

Most companies have either no "mobile" version of their website, or if they do it's really just a smaller version of the same site. The latter is a little better option, but it's still not very effective.

As far as the first problem - having no mobile-specific version of your website - this makes it extremely likely that someone searching for more information will simply leave the page and look for another site that's more friendly.

Look at this website for Southwest Airlines, for example:

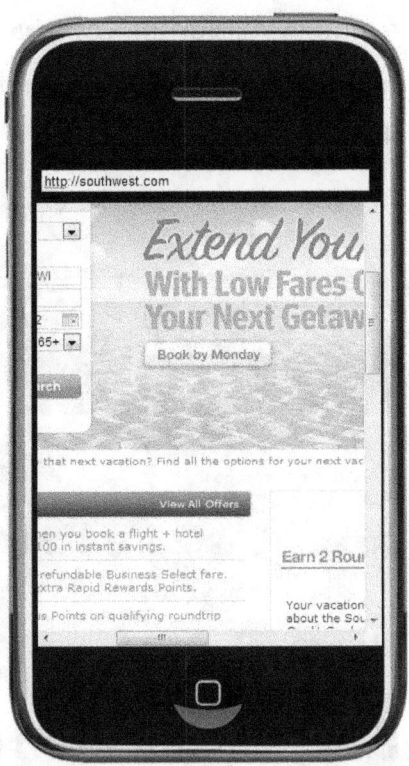

This is what a "regular" website looks like on a typical smartphone. It's practically impossible to read, and even if someone zooms in to see what's there, it's still not going to be very effective. That's crucial considering that, according to one recent survey 61% of Internet users say they won't return to a website they had a hard time accessing with their phone.

Having a mobile-friendly version of your website is the solution. You can see what Southwest's mobile site looks like in this example:

Much easier to read, right?

For small, local businesses, the questions becomes "What are people looking for when they look up a business on their mobile phone?"

Most of the time, they're looking for one of two things - a phone number or an address. They don't want to read the website - they're just trying to call or get to the right location.

Let's look at an example of another effective mobile website:

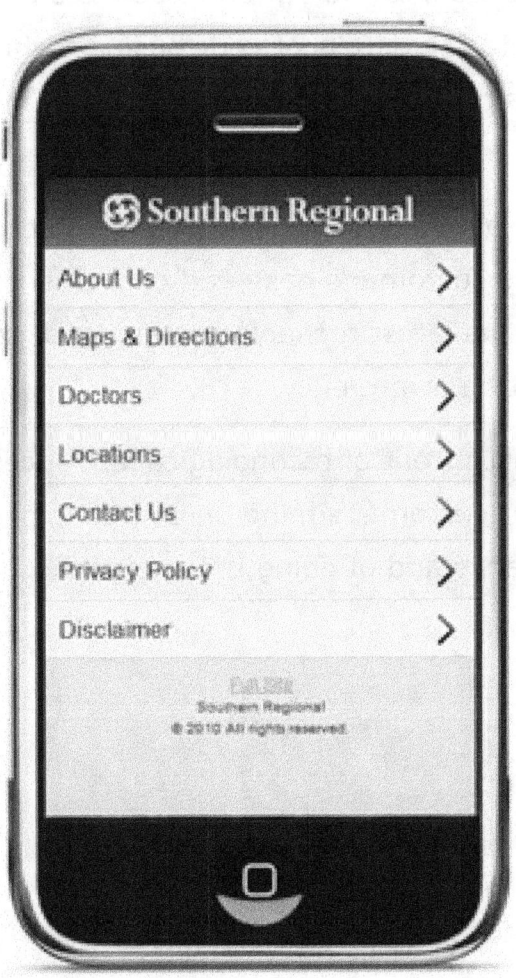

There are many possibilities with mobile websites. Taking advantage of the commonality of GPS function built into smartphones, you may include GPS coordinates on your website, allowing potential customers to click on the link and get directions to your business.

Another option is including contact information on your website so that customer can click a link and automatically have it all loaded into their phone's address book. This quick access to the details of your business should result in many returns from the customer.

It is this sort of *added value* that can fuel the *Perpetuation of Success* explored earlier. It makes you look thoughtful, mindful of the customer's ease and convenience, and in command of the latest technologies—indeed, some that they may not be aware of.

If you are out in front of technological advances, this will create in your customer's mind an overall impression of high competence and of going the extra mile.

Text Messaging

The last area of mobile marketing we'll explore is text messaging, or SMS (short message service). This has experienced huge growth in use. And it's not only younger people who are using it – all generations are.

Local businesses can use text messaging to engage their customers on a much more personal basis than even email marketing can provide.

There are two traits of text messages that set them apart:

• Reach—The phone goes with the person—your customer doesn't have to get to a laptop to see your message.

• Immediacy – People tend to read their texts almost immediately, and on average, much more quickly that e-mails.

These features make texts suited to posting information that doesn't have a long lead time—perhaps you weren't able to get a video together or made limited mention of a particular item a few days in advance. One example would be special promotions. Say a pub has too much inventory of Crazy Jay's Lager, with a new order arriving in two days. If it texts its customers at 4 that afternoon announcing a special on Crazy Jay's tonight and tomorrow night, it can reasonably expect results that night.

This doesn't have to require sending the text to a hundred different phone numbers.

Services are available that will broadcast a text to everyone who has requested to receive them from you. These services let you choose a number, called a Short Code, to use as your point of contact. Your customers just have to send a text to that number to sign up to receive text messages from you whenever you broadcast something out.

You can even set up an automatic response from these short codes, giving you the ability to offer an incentive to get people to opt into receiving those messages.

For example, a restaurant might offer a coupon for a free appetizer on their next visit by texting the word "appie" to their short code number. When the customer sends the text, they get a response virtually instantly with the details of how to get the free appetizer. This can be as simple as "Show this message to your server on your next visit to claim your free appetizer." Thus, each time you broadcast a text message, they will receive it instantly.

Coupon Sites

"Deal of the day" sites like Groupon and Living Social are another highly effective way to reach people through their mobile devices. You can advertise a special offer on these sites, which have apps for smartphones like the iPhone and Blackberry.

These apps offer what is known as "push" notifications of new specials. This works very similar to a text message – when a new offer is posted, the app displays a message on the phone.

Let's look at Groupon.com, the largest and probably best-known coupon site. Groupon bills itself as an opportunity for customers to get amazing discounts—it's not the place for you to offer 10-15%, but instead discounts of about 70% or higher. You list a special offer of some type with Groupon, which then sends it out to its members via e-mail or mobile apps. A user decides whether or not to sign up for it. Once enough people sign up for the offer, it goes into effect. This means you are guaranteed dozens of customers, rather than a few.

Groupon encourages people who have signed up for an offer to mention it via Facebook, Twitter, etc., to help ensure it will gain enough customers to go into effect.

Articles on Internet marketing tend to characterize attracting new customers as the main benefit of Groupon. This is a well-known use of coupons, of course. A study commissioned by—exercise some scepticism here—Groupon itself, found that 91% of owners were able to attract new customers with their promotion.

When deciding whether or not to use a tool such as Groupon, one thing to consider is that there is some negative perception of the site and its services. A somewhat common problem has been that businesses have simply been overwhelmed by an influx of customers coming in for highly-discounted items. There is a perception among employees—who weren't the ones to decide to offer these discounts—that customers don't spend money beyond the discounted item, and as bargain-hunters, may not tip, if applicable.

Further, Groupon has been the center of controversies involving Internet commerce tax and an alleged violation of gift card laws.

You may exercise some caution and do some research, also considering the various coupon sites, such as ScoutMob and Buywithme.

Keys To An Effective Website

Having discussed many tools and services and ways of reaching your customers you may not have tried before, it's important to not lose site on something with which you already are familiar: your own website.

One main function of some of the numerous tools and services described above is to drive traffic to your site. What users see when they get there is, of course, crucial. Here are some key responsibilities of your website:

• Educating your audience

• Building relationships with your audience

• Generating leads and sales

• Branding your company

• Establishing your expertise in your industry

Designing Your Website

One mistake a lot of companies make is trying to crowd too much information onto the home page of their site. This can result in a page with too many tabs and links, too many categories, a generally cluttered feel. It can cause the user to be unsure which link to click. It may ultimately drive them aware.

You want people to be able to find what they want within 5 seconds of landing on your website if at all possible.

Thus, think use the homepage as a sort of "directory" for the rest of the site. It is not there to provide the text of articles, more than one or two embedded videos, or the meat of much information the users will navigate to. Instead in should grab the visitor's attention and provide a few logical and logically-organized links for navigation. The design should be clean and easy-to-read.

Try to look at your website from the perspective of a stranger to your company—someone unfamiliar with your offerings. This will give you the proper perspective for designing a website that can educate your visitors, and that, most importantly, will be user friendly. An effective way to do it is to create a customer "avatar," a model for your typical customer.

Create a fictional customer modelled after your typical client. Give her a name, an age, income, and other demographic information. The more complete this avatar is, the better.

While writing content for designing or re-designing it, aim for that highly-defined avatar. This should streamline your content, make it all as relevant as possible, and make it user-friendly.

Email Marketing

"66% of those surveyed said they had made a purchase because of a marketing message received through email."
- ExactTarget, "2008 Channel Preference Survey"

As far as personal connection and interaction goes, one of the best ways to achieve this in the digital realm is email.

One of the most critical things you should be doing on your website is implementing a lead capture form—a form in which your customer types his name and email address, agreeing to receive email updates from you.

Every page on your website should have an opt-in form where people can sign up to receive your emails. You can also have capture forms for specific offers:

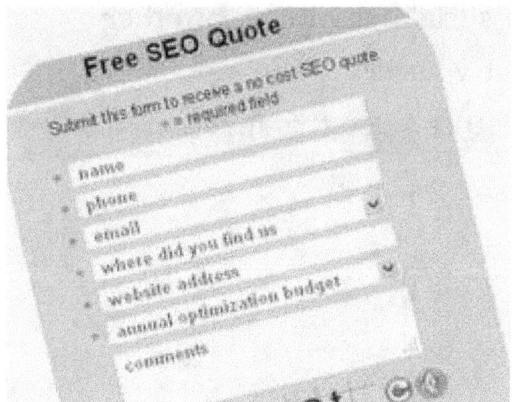

Hubspot Blog offers some savvy tips for creating the best Lead Capture forms. They make the very sharp point that short lead capture forms like the one above—and they can be even shorter—will probably get more responses overall. However, longer ones, asking for information such as age, education level, what sorts of emails the customer might like to receive, will be, of course, better leads.

Another key consideration is privacy. It's a good idea to use a third-party security system and have a link to the security policy highly visible near the form.

Hubspot also recommends using a button for submission that is *not* labelled "Submit," but instead something like, for emails in general, "go," or "yes, please," and something more specific for particular offers, such as "begin the savings."

As with communication via social networking or other methods, you need not limit yourself to the most basic information with emails. You can use this medium for:

• Upcoming promotions

• Coupons

• Newsletter

• How-to information

• Anything else that would be relevant to your customers

Unlike flyers or other types of advertising, email doesn't have a per-message cost. Whether you send 20 emails a month or 2,000 emails a month, your cost isn't going to change by much, if at all.

What that means for you is that you can send an email as often as you like, and you can do it on short notice. So if you have a special event coming up or some other special promotion that you want to remind your customers about, it's just a matter of writing a quick email and sending it out to them a couple of days ahead of the event.

Using an "autoresponder" makes this process a lot less labor-intensive.

Autoresponders are tools that queue emails you load into them and send them out on a schedule you create. The emails go out when scheduled, once a week, whatever you choose.

For example, a dentist's office could send a reminder via email a day or two ahead of a scheduled appointment (not to mention a text message with the same information the day of the appointment), while a car dealer could send a reminder that it's time for the next oil change at the proper time following a customer's last visit.

Remember, too, that email is a two-way communication tool: use it to solicit feedback.

• Ask customers what products or services they want or need that you don't currently offer.

• Solicit feedback and testimonials you can use in future promotions

Sure, you'll get responses from a small percentage of your clientele. But the responses you do get could allow you to make your business so much more responsive to your customers' needs that you could see solid results on the bottom line.

What about people who never visit your website? Many businesses get opt-ins from their in-store customers. You may do this by displaying a laptop or iPad on which people can enter their name and email address right at the point of sale.

To increase the number of people who sign up to receive your emails, you can offer them some sort of incentive for doing so. This could be something like a free report that will help educate them about the products or services you offer, or it could be some sort of special offer or coupon that gets sent to them automatically after they sign up to receive your emails.

Or you could do both to improve your conversions even further. Offering a free report has another advantage: you can use it to promote all the reasons why a potential customer would want to deal with your business as opposed to your competition.

It gives you the opportunity to explain why your company is their best choice, and what unique benefits you can offer. If you provide them with a report that helps them learn more about what you have to offer them, and then include a bit of a sales pitch at the end, it can generate a lot of new customers for your company.

You could even add a message to the end of every customer receipt or invoice, asking them to sign up for your emails at your website.

Treat this email list as a valuable part of your business – because it is – and promote it anywhere and everywhere you can.

Multiple Methods Of Contact

We've been spending some time talking about getting your customers to agree to be contacted by you. But it doesn't have to be so hard—of course, some of them will want to contact *you.* Your website should make it easy for them to do so, no matter what method of communication they prefer. All the places they can get in touch with you should be easily found when they arrive at your website. This includes things such as:

- Your phone number

- Your address

- Links to other websites like Facebook and Twitter

- A "contact us" form where they can send you a message directly from the website

The more ways you give your customers to contact you, the more likely it is that they will. And different people prefer different methods, so make it easy for each of them to do it the way they want.

If you're really ambitious, and it fits the way you do business, you could even offer a live chat function on your website that lets your visitors chat with someone directly over the internet.

This is similar to a telephone conversation in many ways, except the communication is typed through the chat service instead.

This method of contact won't work for every business, but if you or a staff member is sitting in front of the computer for much of the day, it may work for you. And while it may seem a bit "anti-social" to some people, there are a lot of people who aren't comfortable calling and speaking to you in person or on the phone, but would be very comfortable chatting over the internet instead.

Promotional Strategies

Press Releases

The first major promotional/public relations method we'll explore is the press release. This is a short document meant to read just like a story in a local newspaper, and in the case of businesses, possibly in a trade publication. When journalists or editors receive press releases, they sometimes run them as-is, and sometimes label them "press release" or "news release," to signify that the story is coming from the horse's mouth and didn't involve reporting.

Sometimes journalists will edit or change these slightly, either because shortcomings with grammar, spelling, or syntax necessitate this, or from a journalistic ethic that resists allowing a PR person to be able to tell their own story without any "objective," third-party intervention.

The story then very well may run in a local newspaper or magazine. There's also the matter of online news sites. If your press release makes one of these, you of course appear in search results and have a clickable link to your website (as opposed to a print link that may or may not appear in a newspaper article)

that will drive traffic to your site, which in turn should help your site rise in search results. There are a number of press release services that will distribute your press release to various newspapers, websites and other media outlets. Some of the most effective include:

• PRWeb.com

• Webwire.com

• Marketwire.com

• PR.com

• WirePRNews.com

PRWeb.com, in particular, promises to get your news releases posted on the high-profile news sites such as Yahoo! News and Google News. They use SEO techniques to help get you the best-possible place in rankings. The cost of these services varies, depending on the number of outlets they broadcast to and what other additional services they provide.

Press releases may seem intimidating at first, and it may be unclear what to write about. One key strategy in getting started is to keep a notebook of business stories appearing in local publications—what sorts of business activities are considered news? The news pages of publications, after all, are not for advertising, even though from your point of view, any publicity you can get absolutely does translate into advertising.

The key is to be creative and to orient your mind around what is newsworthy. On the one hand, it's important to create a high degree of relevance and a feel of "news" (as opposed to "self-promotion") to your releases. However, that doesn't mean you should limit yourself and wait for something huge before getting the word out. Local newspapers, particularly, pride themselves on as much local coverage (as opposed to national stories from wire services) as possible. They may be short-staffed, with journalists scrambling around, unable to give attention to everything breaking nearby, and thus more than happy for a well-written, succinct, relevant release.

Topics for Press Releases

• New products – The public happily accepts new products and innovations as newsworthy stories rather than as self-serving promotion. If your company is manufacturing a new product or rolling out a substantially new line, the innovation of this and its place in a culture in which products are highly-valued, will be the angle

• Major changes – Obviously, if your company is under new management (you're now taking over) or has been involved in a merger or acquisition, or a new location, this is, again, very useful information the public will want. It allows your company to be noticed without (or in addition to) paid advertisement or any words or phrases associated with sales pitches

• Awards or other professional achievements – If you have won an award from the Chamber of Commerce, a state or regional organization, or a trade organization, write about it. If you made a presentation or participated in a panel at a trade convention, write about it.

• Innovative or unique business strategies – I recently saw a news story about a pizza restaurant that fuelled its delivery cars with leftover oil from its deep fryers! This is news because of the alternative energies angle, and it shows local people being innovators. It's also just interesting as a slice-of-life story. If you have a way of marketing, staffing, cutting costs, etc., not only would a local paper be interested, but trade journals would as well. This kind of story would do well in the online environment in addition to locally.

• Community involvement or activism – Recall Julie, our fearless candy shop owner from the Facebook section. She was sure to post pictures of her involvement in charities, fundraisers, etc. using social media. Your competitors may do this, and they may get mired in the mindset that the Internet is all there is. But if you've donated funds to a scholarship or donated supplies or equipment to a school, it's worth writing a press release. Again, you aren't saying word one about any product or discount offers here. Rather you're letting people know your business exists and that its owner is generous and community-minded.

Quick Press Release Tips

First off, if you got B minuses in high school English, you will probably need help with preparing clean copy that won't turn off the staff at the media organizations. You may write the release originally and have it edited, or you may outline it and give instructions for someone else. It's a short document—it *must* be succinct and to the point—so an employee with better-than-average writing skills should be able to get it submission-ready in an hour or so. If you feel the need to amp things up a little, it shouldn't be hard to find a writer via craigslist, a temp agency, or by contacting the Journalism or English department at your local university.

Assuming you'll be doing the work yourself, it may not be a bad idea to research some methods first. You can use Google for this, but may wish to be a bit more thorough and check out a book on journalism from a library. Books aimed at journalists will apply to you. However, these tips may suffice:

The biggest issues are brevity and clarity. Include only absolutely necessary information and write with the clarity of a set of instructions you'd write telling your spouse how to tivo your favorite television show.

Use the **W**ho **W**hat **W**here **W**hy approach, and use the old journalism institution, the inverted pyramid structure, wherein the most important information appears at the top, with the pyramid narrowing to finer details as the article progresses. With the most important info first, not only will readers (including editors at the publication) understand why they should keep reading, but editorial staff can quickly and easily cut the release to meet space limitations, eliminating just the minor details.

Gregg Laskoski, writing for the media magazine *Tactics,* counsels to explicitly explain who is impacted by this news, and similarly, to anticipate questions that may arise and to answer these.

If you distribute press releases on a regular basis, you will not only be more likely to get noticed by one or more media outlets, you will also get SEO (Search Engine Optimization) benefits that can help your website rank higher in the search engines, and ultimately generate more traffic.

We'll look at SEO in more detail shortly.

Video Distribution

Whereas the traditional media—those you approach with content hoping to gain space in their pages—are very important because of the prestige given to them, as we've touched on previously, most of what this book is about is do-it-yourself methods that allow you to short-circuit this system and go straight to your audience.

Having briefly mentioned video in the context of Google Places and Facebook, we're now ready to go into more detail, not only about places for video distribution, but some techniques and strategies for its use.

As we begin, let's take a minute to remember the concept of Perpetuation of Success, creating an aura of success and professionalism that will only lead to more success. Video is one of your key weapons in this theatre of battle. We are still early enough in the realm of self-produced videos that they carry with them an aura of being technologically-advanced and creative, or may make people think you have paid someone to make a video for you. Some users may wonder how you did it, and most should unconsciously find your business to be advanced, high-tech, and deluxe.

It's also important to mention that video's properties make is very appealing to your customers:

• No reading involved. Above, we've discussed press releases and other text. There's nothing wrong with text, and sometimes it is the very best medium for your message. Further, all types of media should be used. However, we know that a) people are sent links to all sorts of articles from their friends all the time and b) while using their computers, a lot of people are multi-tasking and may be more receptive to a quick video.

• This is due to the fact that they can watch your video while intermittently getting back to other things on the web. That might seem a bit sad—of course you want your customers' undivided attention—but it's a reality.

• As goes without saying, all sorts of messages are just made for video. Shots of your inventory or your inventory in use are an obvious example. Another is how-to videos.

• Personalization. Putting a face—in many cases, a literal face—to your business can be beneficial. A voice can also help show the human side of your business and keep it from being just a silent bunch of images on a screen. We've been in a multimedia, sound and picture world for far too long to have a website that relies on text, graphics, and still photos.

So, what goes in these videos? Basic advertising functions need not be explained here. Instead, as with the section on Facebook, let's focus on off-the-beaten path videos that can provide value to your customers. It is now increasingly common for businesses to create a variety of informative videos. This is a way to appear in Google results and get traffic to your video, which may be on youtube or another video site (outlined below) and/or embedded in your website. In either case, you'll of course include the URL to your website, as well as other contact information, both in the video itself and adjoining text such as a brief video description.

So, a computer software company could produce a brief video reviewing antivirus software or showing people how to set up a home network. Ultimately, this is meant to get the user who searched for that information to visit your website. If you want to be sure to have some tie-in to one of your products in each video you may do so.

You may also have a video that explains a certain concept that may be confusing to many people. This may include text and pie charts or other graphics you can easily create. You could put together an entire glossary of terms. As is the case with the how-to videos above, not only will this get potential customers on your side by giving them free help, it will establish your expertise. No one believes he/she will find a culinary expert every time she walks into a kitchen supply store in the mall, and certainly not in one of the big chain stores. Your videos and the range of knowledge you share may encourage customers to walk through your doors. They already know you are familiar with a particular product and its uses—they can refer to your video and start the conversation on the same page with you.

Be creative and brainstorm for as many informative or attention-grabbing videos in any way related to your business as you can. If you own a ski shop and are an avid skier, why not post videos of your recent trip to a well-known resort with its lush, powdery snow? If you own an auto body shop, post of video having to do with the NASCAR circuit. If you run a daycare center, shoot a video overview of some of the latest DVD's for children. In all of these cases, you are addressing something your potential customers will be interested in and will search for via Google.

This allows you to cast your net in different areas. You've already posted various content that will come up under searches for "body shop Jamestown, PA." These videos give you a chance to reach people searching for NASCAR, children's DVD's, etc. Of course, they'll also come up under the local business searches because of the inclusion of your business's name and contact information. Having this kind of reach is, of course, even more useful if your product can be bought online, since it will apply to people in all geographic areas.

Of course, there are how-to videos demonstrating your products and services, which can include dramatizations or testimonials from real customers. And as mentioned above, basic information on your product line, prices, special offers—basically, a television commercial. You can also include a video as a welcome to your homepage (but remember to keep the homepage uncluttered) or to other sections of your site. You can also go the route of the photo collage, using JPEG files of pictures of your inventory, most attractive employees, etc., set to music.

How To Produce Videos

If you've never made a video before, that doesn't mean you're not in possession of the tools and skills necessary. If your PC doesn't come with a built-in webcam, you can buy one for roughly twenty-five dollars. Or you can of course use your digital video camera or a similar, portable device. Once you've shot the video, you'll need to upload it to your PC, which is usually done via your video editing software.

PC's come loaded with Windows Movie Maker, free video-editing software. It will import your raw video and allow you to cut it, move clips around, add music, and publish the video to youtube, Facebook, etc., or render as a file such as .avi or .mpeg. For Macs, it's Apple i-movie.

There are other free pieces of software that won't come factory-installed, but which you can download online. Of these, the best is probably AVS Video Editor 6.1. If you are interested in purchasing software, for PC's, Cyberlink Power Director and Corel Video Studio are the best affordable options, with latest versions usually running about $90. MAC users will go with Final Cut Pro.

Retail software will give you more video tracks, so you can have picture-in-picture, split-screen, an image faded into the main image on the screen, etc. It will give you more in the way of special video effects and transitions between shots. However, AVS Video Editor 6.1, for freeware, has a surprising array of transitions and effects. And while Windows Movie Maker frankly works like freeware, you will find it adequate for your videos unless you absolutely need a huge selection of advanced features.

Specific techniques and procedures for editing video are beyond the scope of this book, but here are a few general pointers.

Music is a good nicety, particularly for the intro and outro of the video. Copyright-free music can be found at freemusicarchive.com and other web locations. It can be played over a typical introduction of text on the screen announcing the focus of the video, and probably your business name. I recommend using the most visually-interesting fonts available through your video editor, and taking the time to generally create a good first impression by making the introduction as professional as possible. In short, try to present your business this way

rather than this way

Unless you're absolutely certain the contrary is the case, it's important to try to distance yourself from a "cheesy home movie" feel as possible. This can be done with just a couple of tweaks to the video's saturation, the use of one simple effect, a bit of reverb or other enhancement to the audio, etc.

Publishing Video

Once you've shot and edited your video, you must "render" it, which turns it into a viewable movie, either in flash format (.flv) or a higher-quality format, such as .avi or .mpeg or .mp4, all of which can be embedded on your website or uploaded to youtube. Most video editing programs have a function that uploads videos directly to facebook or youtube, etc. Here's a screenshot from PowerDirector:

But there's also the matter of rendering the video in a format that will be stored on your hard drive for permanent use and for use in other venues. Youtube, famous as it is, is far from the only corner of the Internet devoted to video hosting.

Other popular video sites include:

Vimeo.com

Dailymotion.com

Veoh.com

Justin.tv

Buzznet.com

Collegehumor.com

Ustream.tv

Revver.com

Of these, vimeo and DailyMotion are the most mainstream and best known. However, while you certainly want users to find you videos on these sites and through Google Video, etc., a lot of traffic to the videos will come through places you've embedded them, such as blogs, Pinterest, Facebook, and your business webpage. Therefore, one factor in decided which services to use is to look at how easy it is to embed videos from them to Facebook and other venues.

Article Distribution

Article distribution is another highly effective way to reach your customers online. This differs from press releases because they are not necessarily news about your business, and are not submitted to traditional media for possible publication. Instead, they are published online at sites with built-in traffic for articles. In most cases, there is not an acceptance or rejection process—you open an account and submit an article and it appears on the site in the next day or two. Rejection or removal of articles would become an issue only if you posted inappropriate content.

Sites to submit articles include:

Ezinearticles.com

GoArticles.com

Articlesbase.com

WebProNews.com

ArticleDashboard.com

Article-buzz.com

Here's a screenshot of the homepage of Ezinearticles.com, listing recently-added articles:

Retail Property Managers - Tenant Selection Tips for Better

When it comes to selecting a new tenant for retail property or a retail shop clear considerations and factors to... more

Got Jerks? Get Help

Got any jerks in your life? You know the type. The ones who think they know it to a word you say, the ones who push and push until you can't take it, or the victim but the last... more

Empaths Working With Ascended Masters

An empath is one who is keenly aware of energy around them. Some ar karma with the physical body and this is draining them. Learn how to work realms of consciousness to accomplish... more

3 Workplace Communication Mistakes Every Woman in Scier Technology Should Avoid

Excellent communication skills are a necessity for any woman who wants t ahead in the fields of science,... more

Tenant Advocacy Business for Commercial Real Estate Ager

Tenant advocacy work remains a significant and specialised part of the con Those agents that choose to... more

Italian Pasta Salad With Pepperoni, Mozzarella Cheese, and

Macaroni salad has long been a staple of American cuisine. It still is, only n and nutritional value. This... more

Commercial Real Estate Agents - Prospecting Letter Strateg

When you work as an agent in commercial real estate, there are various ty used. Importantly you should use the... more

Note how closely these articles conform to the ideas for videos, above. They discuss a particular topic someone might be interested in, giving help and useful information to a reader, and thus demonstrating and establishing some expertise for you.

With your article you will include a short bio at the end, which describes your company and links to your website.

The link in your bio has two benefits:

•   Readers will click on the link to visit your website, and once they do they can sign up for your email list, read more about your company or anything else that you offer on your site.

•   The link helps your website rank higher in Google and other search engines, so the more articles you distribute, the better you will rank when people are searching for local businesses.

The real power of these article sites is in the syndication features they offer. Most of these sites let other websites use your article on their site, as long as they leave your bio intact. As other sites syndicate your article, you will get even more opportunities to reach your customers as well as more and more backlinks helping to push your website up in the search engine rankings.

Being listed as the author of so many articles pertaining to your business will go a long way in establishing expertise, and contribute to your Perpetuation of Success.

Images

Above we've discussed posting photos on Facebook. However, there are many sites that are devoted to photo sharing. Placing your photos in more than one venue is key. It's similar to what we discussed with articles—putting your information where your users will find it is absolutely crucial. Once you've taken a sharp picture that reflects well on your site, don't skimp on broadcasting it. Some of the top photo sites are:

• Flickr.com

• Instagram.com

• Photobucket.com

• Imageshack.com

• Imgur.com

• Picasa.com

• Smugmug.com

Naturally, this kind of marketing is best for businesses with very visual products or services: interior designers, artists, furniture sellers, auto body shops, hair stylists, etc.

To repeat a point so important it can't be stressed enough, while these photo-sharing sites may not be geared for local marketing, having your photos out there on these sites will cause you to appear in Google Images results. It is becoming increasingly common for a horizontal column of these results to appear in the midst of organic Google results, as opposed to the traditional place on the left column of the page. Even if your business doesn't necessarily translate well into pictures, there are reasons you might want to distribute images to these sites.

It's very easy to post your company logo this way—when a searcher sees your company logo in the search results, you'll stand out and be more memorable.

All these things make dealing with your company a little easier for your customers, and when you add them all up, it can make a big difference.

Paid Advertising

So far, we've been discussing guerrilla marketing, diy (do-it-yourself) marketing, however you'd like to describe it. Many new avenues have been opened that can eliminate or reduce your advertising budget. This could absolutely save a fledgling business that otherwise may not be able to get into the black and would otherwise join the ranks of businesses that fail in the first year. Free advertising and promotion are too readily available to pass up.

However, many businesses plan to spend money on advertising, which is a more surefire and less labor-intensive way of getting your word out.

This section will explore various methods and venues for paid advertising:

- Pay per click (PPC) ads

- Banner ads

- Facebook ads

Pay per click ads are one of the most cost effective. These are the "sponsored ads" that are displayed at the top and right of the search results on Google, Yahoo and Bing.

A business pays to have these sponsored ads displayed next to search results for certain keywords. The business owner makes a bid for keywords she is interested in, auction style. This determines the price of the ad, per click. As the name implies, you pay only when someone clicks on your sponsored ad. Rates per click range from from a few cents to several dollars, depending on what industry you are in and what keywords you're bidding on.

More than one business will win a bid for a particular set of keywords, and thus have their ads displayed. One of the factors determining which business is listed at the top of the page is how high the owner bid for the keywords. However, there are other factors as well—particular when dealing with Google, it can get into some pretty heavy calculus. But let's look at getting started.

Your company may provide various services and may stock hundreds of products. You may decide to focus on just a few of these to advertise via pay-per-click. That's because of the keyword structure, the ads being tied to certain results.

For example, if you were in the tool rental business you might bid on some of the following keywords:

Toledo tool rentals

Toledo power drill rental

Toledo mitre saw rental

The idea is to be specific, picking your battles. While "Toledo tool rentals" does refer to your business in general, the other two stick to specific combinations of keywords, anticipating what users may search via Bing or Google, etc. But, note that we didn't use "tool rentals." The reason might seem obvious—you need to specify an area. However, it is possible to have your ads displayed only to users near you. The problem with those keywords is they will be too expensive and bid on by far too many users. That is also the logic by which "power drill rental" is better—more specific, niche keywords will cost you lest. This is true the smaller your city, or, to be more precise, the less competitors are bidding. It's all about honing in, focusing tightly. If you strategize carefully, you can get the best results, and thus the best value for your dollar.

Another thing to keep in mind is that PPC ads are particular potent for businesses that sell online. You are paying when someone clicks on your ad—if that click not only tells her about your business but allows for a purchase on the spot, you're getting the most value.

Conversions

And that brings us next to our next concept related to using and getting the most out of PPC ads: conversions. A conversion is the act of someone not just clicking on your ad, but doing something beneficial for you company upon going to your site. Most people would probably agree that a purchase is the ultimate conversion, but it isn't the only one. Filling out a lead-capture form to receive e-mails and sending you an inquiry or requesting some free service available are all examples.

The point is that while you *are* paying for the click and not the conversion, it is clearly the conversion you are looking for. Now, in the case of a brick and mortar business with a web presence, a person could visit your website, leave without any of the aforementioned conversions, and come into your store and spend forty dollars. More on that in a minute. But let's look at how to consider your conversions when deciding how much to spend on PPC advertising. Internet marketing company portent.com offers the following formula:

Be sure that the amount you spend per click is less than the profit you earn per click.

So, the rate you pay must be less than:

conversion rate * total clicks * profit per conversion

In this case, you are considering conversions to be only actual purchases, because those are the only ones associated with a profit.

Say you're paying $1.00 per click. You get 200 clicks per month and 2% of those lead to a sale. You average $10.00 per profit.

So you have

.02 * 200 * 10=40

You are making $40 from this PPC campaign, while spending $200 for it. If you can't find a way to get more conversions, you'll need to close this campaign and bid on less expensive keywords.

Getting back to the idea of walk-in "conversions," people spending money in person, if you have four people who said "hey, I saw your ad online," while making a purchase, you may adjust these numbers a bit. The main takeaway is to pay attention to data on conversions—mere clicks are not the ultimate goal.

There's also the matter of the Quality Score. This is another factor that affects whether or not your ad is at the top of results pages, along with how high you bid. Yahoo and Google both implement a quality score, looking at according to portent.com, the ad itself, its performance, and the quality of the page to which the ad links. One important consideration here is that the keyword you are bidding on should appear in the ad.

Banner Advertising

Banner ads are large graphical ads placed on websites. They come in many sizes, ranging from a small vertical banner (120x240 pixels) to the more common full banner (486x60 pixels). You can work directly with websites you find beneficial for your ads or purchase ads through a company designed for this, called an ad network. Ad networks find relevant websites for your ads, decide which cities the ads are placed in, etc. By far the largest and most powerful ad network is one you've probably heard of, Google AdWords. Another giant is Yahoo! Publisher Network, with others including DoubleClick and Flycast.

Another method is swapping ads. This means swapping space on your site for space on someone else's site. You may not wish to enter into something like this with a direct competitor, but doing so with tangentially related businesses could work. For example, a plumbing business would exchange ads with local electricians, realtors, contractors under the logic that someone seeking one of these would be seeking others. You'd arrange one of these partnerships through contacting the relevant parties.

A more formal way to do this is to join a Banner Exchange Program. This involves going through a third-party services setting up exchanges. You receive banner ads from other businesses, display them by pasting in the code on your site, and your ads go out to other sites.

Examples of companies running these programs are:

- LinkExchange

- BannerSwap

- SmartClicks

Physically creating the banner ad isn't terribly difficult, though it requires a bit of knowledge of HTML and some skill with graphics. Many ads consist of still images, while some involve animated gifs. If you are interested in sophisticated banners, you'll probably have to search online for companies specializing in creating banners.

You may explore the option of offering "finder's fees" for any referrals that you get as a result of another local business. You can set up a system that will track any new customers who click through from an ad on one of your partner businesses' website and wind up contacting you. You can then pay the person who referred them a finder's fee. If you set up these types of partnerships with several other complementary businesses, it can work out well for everyone involved without taking anything away from their own bottom line.

Banner advertising can be very effective, but for local business purposes you need to be sure that you are able to control where your ads get displayed. If you're an electrician in Portland, Oregon there's really no point in having your ad shown to someone who is surfing the web in Sarasota, Florida.

Facebook Ads

While Facebook always seems to be the subject of one controversy or another, it is still used by just about everyone and is generally regarded as a good place for your advertising dollars. Besides the fact that Facebook is one of the most famous entities on Earth, one of the draws for advertisers is the high level of customization. Mark Zuckerberg and crew offer what no other known advertising venue does, and that is to use their ad criteria to finely tailor who sees your ads.

You are able to address each of the following criteria:

• Age

•Gender

•Country

•State

• City

• Zip Code

• Language

• Broad Interest

• Precise Interest

• Connections

• Friends of Connections

- Workplace

- Relationship

- Language

- Education

Here, via socialfresh.com, is a graph showing the popularity of each:

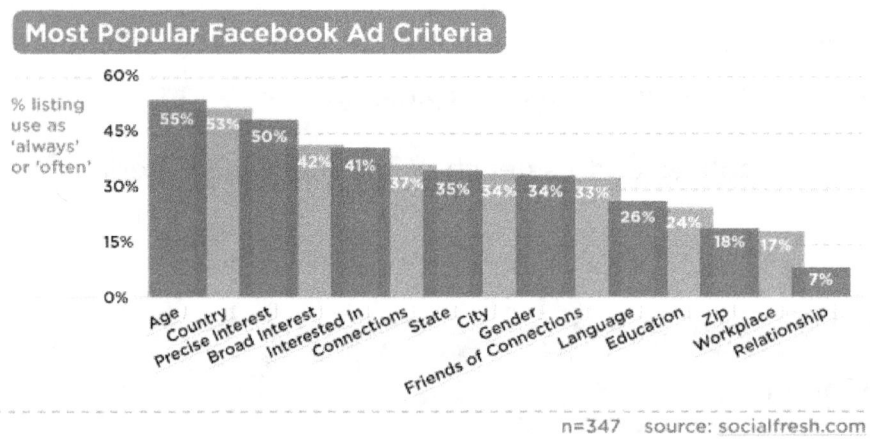

I'll go through and comment on a few of these, pointing out some things that aren't self-explanatory.

Geography -- In the U.S. you can choose any of the above geographical filters, sending ads only to people in that area. That is, you can place an ad only for people in 21532, or only in a city, etc. You can further narrow it to just women in that area-- if you own a gym or fitness club, you could create an ad that would target women between the ages of 35 and 50 who live in your city. You can also send the ad to just those women who have a college degree.

Precise Interests – What's better, you can also send the ad just to those women who say, on the information on their profile page, they are fans of a particular workout TV show or who list working out as a hobby or interest. Those of you with facebook accounts have probably gotten ads on the right side of your news feed page that seem eerily appropriate to you.

Connections – This is similar to precise interests. It allows you to target users according to their connection to a particular Facebook page. If you'd like to target ads to people who are fans or friends of or members of a group page for, say, Jenny Craig, you can do that. You can even *exclude* people on that basis.

Keep in mind, of course, that once you've crafted a particular ad for a particular audience, there's no reason you can't craft another ad targeted at a different group.

Now that we've looked at options available for whom your ad goes to, let's quickly outline the two main types of ads:

1) Marketplace Ad. This is the standard advertisement, touting your business and its products or services. You choose your audience criteria, described above, and then get started with your ad. You supply the ad copy and some graphics, and Facebook generates the ad. Here's a screenshot from Facebook's self-serve tool:

Step 3: Design an Engaging Ad

Create multiple versions of your ads with different images and body copy to find out which combinations are most effective.

Here are some tips for creating effective ads:

- Include your business or Page name, a question, or key information the title

- Provide a clear action to take in the body copy, and highlight the benefits

- Use a simple, eye-catching image that is related to your body copy title

- Target different audiences to determine which groups are most responsive to your ads

Visit your **Ads Manager** to update your ads regularly with new images and body copy to prevent them from going stale

2) The second kind of ad is a Sponsored Story. Now, despite the name, this ad is roughly the same size and shape as a marketplace ad, and isn't really a "story." It's an ad that says that one of your friends "liked" a particular business, interacted with your business app, check into your business as a location, etc. This is, of course, using a potential customer's friend as digital word of mouth.

With either of these kinds of ads, remember, you are supplying "the creative," which means a jpeg (of a customer sipping you coffee, of a forklift your business rents, etc.) or some other media. Because these are very small ads, one must be careful in selecting one of these images. Matthew Creamer, writing for *Advertising Age* gives brief and simple guidelines: "the image needs to have an obvious focal point, the brand needs to be clear and the ad needs to fit with the brand's personality." If the image you are shooting for your photo isn't foregrounded enough and presented crisply, in sharp focus, viewed at roughly 100 x 160 pixels, it may be hard to even identify, much less to be memorable or persuasive.

Worth a mention is a promotion offered by American Express. Businesses using the credit card can earn Membership Points and cash them in for credits toward Facebook ads in increments of $50, $100, and $250.

Search Engine Optimization

A very important part of any online presence is being visible as high in search results as possible. Thus, while a lot of what has been discussed so far relates to Search Engine Optimization, we do need to discuss this concept explicitly.

Search Engine Optimization (SEO) is achieved through many steps, but can be defined, holistically, as doing everything necessary to make your site appear as high in the non-paid (or "organic") results of a search engine. It is comprised of understanding how search engines work, what keywords users type into search engines, etc. Some of the best ways to optimize your website, which we'll discuss in detail below, are:

• finding which keywords are most searched and including these in your web page titles and descriptions

• drumming up "backlinks" as described above (through articles, Web 2.0 content, etc.) to improve the rank of your site in SE results.

• carefully attending to tags and other material to remove barriers that prevent your site from raning high.

First, let's look at keyword optimization. This involves finding out which keywords relevant to your business are most commonly used in search engines.

Fortunately, you have access to various tools to approach this scientifically. One is the Google Keyword Tool. It's designed to aid Google Adwords advertisers decide what keywords to bid on for their ads. But it works just as well for keyword optimization.

Let's look at a quick example. This screenshot shows a search for "bellingham plumbers" (Bellingham is a city in Washington with a population of about 80,000 and 200,000 in the metro area).

Keyword ideas (59)

Keyword	Competition	Global Monthly Searches	Local Monthly Searches
bellingham plumber		720	590
plumbers in seattle		1,600	1,600
bellingham plumbers		880	720
plumbers bellingham		880	720
plumber bellingham		720	590
plumber		1,000,000	450,000
plumbers		673,000	368,000
plumbing bellingham		590	480
plumbers in bellingham wa		73	73
plumbing contractors		33,100	27,100
bellingham plumbing		590	480
plumbing questions		4,400	2,900
plumbing repair		27,100	22,200
plumber seattle		2,400	2,400
plumber in bellingham		320	260
plumbing problems		12,100	8,100
plumbing services		49,500	22,200
bellingham map		3,600	2,900
pex plumbing		12,100	12,100
emergency plumbing		18,100	8,100

These are just a few of the keywords that the tool returns, and you can see what people are searching for and roughly how many times each keyword gets searched every month.

Take a look at the keyword phrase "bellingham plumber" (the one we searched for here). It gets 590 local monthly searches. That's 590 potential customers who are searching for that term every month, on average.

You can see several other variations on the main keyword we searched for:

- Bellingham plumbers

- Plumber bellingham

- Plumbers bellingham

- Plumbers in bellingham wa

If you owned a plumbing business in Bellingham, you would want to work these variations into the content on your website to help improve your SEO and get ranked higher in the results when people are searching for those terms.

Here is how to do that.

Title Tags – When you, your webmaster, or the company creating your website are putting things together, you must create a title for the each page. This is not the URL, but text, such as "Dave's Rentals—Best Construction Tools," or "Anna's Designs—For Home or Office." These used to appear at the top of web browsers, but now fill the tabs atop browsers:

Here, an abbreviated version of the title tag for NBA.com and iye.com, the website for the record store In Your Ear, are shown. What's most important here is that this information will, of course, be used in search engine results.

The idea is to use the keywords, such as Bellingham Plumbers, in the title tag. So if your business is Angostine & Sons, your title tag might be "Angostine & Sons, Bellingham's Most Affordable Plumbers."

Best practices in SEO include the following:

• Keep it short –try to keep it to less than 75 characters. Otherwise, the search engine results will cut off the description given in this tag and use an ellipsis ("…"), making it hard for the user to read.

• Put important keywords near the beginning of the tag. This will be helpful not only for ranking but for motivating a user to click on them in search results.

Meta Tags—These are the words and phrases that describe your website. Specifically, Meta Decription Tags are the largest source of the "snippet," which is the little blurb under the title tag in search engine results:

NBA.com
www.nba.com/
The official site of the **National Basketball Association**. Includes news, features, multimedia, player profiles, chat transcripts, schedules and statistics.

The key here is that you can, of course, place crucial keywords in this description. Keywords searched by a user will be bolded in results—I above, I searched for National Basketball Association. If I would have searched for NBA players, the word "player" in the snippet would be bolded. While these don't affect the rank directly, if they are chosen carefully, they will lead to clicks on your page.

The other place to be sure to have the best keywords is in page content itself—articles, descriptions and listings of products, etc. If razor scooters is a phrase trending in your area, and your bike shop offers them, be sure to include text or labelled photos and various pages of your site mentioning this. Using keywords strategically, enough to get search engine results, is effective and accepted practice. Until you get to the point of overusing them or using them in a way that could be considered misleading, you'll be fine, behaving ethically and not running afoul of the latest search engine techniques designed to catch this.

Search Engine Optimization involves content you post on other sites, like press releases, videos, images and various other types of content. The links that point back to your website from these places will help your site's ranking improve.

In addition to finding and using proper keywords, generating links back to your site is a form of SEO, working to bump your site to the top of results. Part of the calculation that Google and other search engines use to rank your website is the number of links, and the "power" of the websites they're on.

For example, if you a link pointed to your website from a site like CNN.com it would be considerably more valuable to your ranking than a link from Bobsmufflers.com.

There are various ways you can generate these links to your website. We've already discussed some of them, when we looked at media distribution. Articles, videos and various other media can include links to your website, so as you distribute them to more and more places you will generate more and more links back to your site.

You can also buy links on other websites. This is essentially a form of advertising, but instead of paying for another site to display your banner or paying for clicks on Google or Facebook, you're paying another site to link back to yours with your goal being better rankings.

The idea here is to think of search results as exactly what they are, advertising. Space atop search engine results—including the "organic" results—is prime real estate. However important and valuable it is to buy traditional advertising, it is equally important, and more economical, to invest in catapulting to the top of Search Engine results.

Getting involved with some of sites we've discussed earlier in the book can also help generate more links to your site. If you're active on Facebook and Twitter, you can use those sites to link to your website. Review sites like Yelp.com will also have links back to your website.

You can even set up multiple websites of your own, each with a very narrow focus. All of them can link back to your main site, helping to push its rankings up. For example, you might set up "minisites" for different product lines that you sell, or different services that you offer – each with a very specific focus. And these sites won't just be useful for linking back to your main website, they can also generate even more visitors and new customers as people find them in the search engines and various other places.

As you can see, many of these strategies work in tandem with one another. Media distribution doesn't just get your name out there, it helps with SEO. Being active on Facebook and Twitter doesn't just give your customers another way to contact you, it also helps your website rank better.

The more you market your business online, the more your efforts will perpetuate themselves and lead to exponential success. But keep in mind that SEO is not a project to be completed via one-time effort. You can ease back on the amount of content that you are distributing to various places once you've made an initial push to get your site ranked, but to maintain those rankings you'll need to do a certain amount of this on an ongoing basis. Otherwise, if your competitors are also improving their SEO, they could leapfrog your site in the rankings.

Tracking Your Results

Internet marketing affords great opportunities for tracking an analysing your results. This allows you to ascertain, with some precision, where youcustomers are coming from and which ad sources are most and least profitable.

You can even trace these sources to specific messages or media. For example, if you post a video on YouTube, you can code a special tracking link into it so you know exactly how many people end up visiting your website as a result.

There are many tracking services available to you, ranging from free solutions to hundreds, or even thousands of dollars per month. One of the most effective is actually free to use – Google Analytics.

Google Analytics will track visitors coming to your website, where they're coming from and many other things. It will even tell you what keywords people searched for when they found your website in the search results.

This data can be invaluable to you because over time you can analyse it and work it back into your website to get even better results.

For example, using our Bellingham plumber example again, when you analyze your site's data you might find that you're getting traffic from Google for the phrase "bellingham plumbing and heating" – a phrase you didn't do any optimization for.

Seeing that, you could hop over to Google and see just where your site ranks for that term. Let's say you find it towards the bottom of the page, maybe spot 7 or 8 (there are normally ten results shown on each page).

From this research, you now know two important things – people are already finding your site after searching "Bellingham plumbing and heating," and that you could quite likely improve your ranking by doing a little bit of SEO for that phrase.

You might write a new article to add to your website that uses the phrase "bellingham plumbing and heating" or you might just add it to a page or two that are already on the site.

This painless amount of work would drive traffic to your site. Google Analytics doesn't just track your visitors, however – it can also track the actions those visitors take once they arrive at your website.

For example, if you have a lead capture form on your site to get people's name and email address so you can follow up with them in the future, you can track the people who actually sign up for your email list. With Google Analytics, you're able to track all the way from the click on one of your ads through to someone signing up to receive your emails.

And from there, you could use tracking codes to identify those people when they come into your place of business or contact you for more information. This lets you track the exact cost per customer by calculating your advertising cost versus the number of people who wind up doing business with you.

Here are some other analytical tools:

• Clicky – One thing this service offers that Google Analytics does not is click-stream data. Generally though, it's bigger on ease of use and simplicity than on variety of features

• FoxMetrics – This tool specializes in tracking "events," or particular actions such as newsletter views, software installations, etc.

• MixPanel – One of the key benefits of this tool is its ability to track conversion funnels in real time.

Whichever tool you use, it is important to analyse your results.

Review

Now that we've come to the end and have explored an array of concepts that may be new to you, let's condense the information and review.

₪ Google Tools ₪

At the opening of the book, we discussed how important search engines are and how important it is to be found in their results pages. Because Google is the leader of search engines, using its various components is important and effective.

Google Places – This important tool places your business on a map, which is a distinctive, eye-catching part of a search results page. It involves a page for your business, with many features, including customer reviews.

₪ Customer Reviews ₪

Customer Reviews, via Google Pages or review sites are becoming increasingly crucial. Yelp.com and other review sites get millions of unique visitors per month, and more and more people report that they consider user reviews to be important. Being aware of reviews of your business and responding proactively to them is important.

₪ Social Networking ₪

One component any online interaction is the user feeling part of some community. Social Networking is the marketing medium that allows you to attend to that. It also allows you to be in control of your message with no gatekeeper of any kind.

₪ Mobile Marketing ₪

Mobile marketing is important now and will probably be crucial five years from now. The biggest key is to be sure that you have a site designed expressly for mobile devices: give easy-to-find, basic information on your homepage.

₪ General Website Design ₪

If it's important to drive traffic to your business's website, isn't it also important for that traffic to find something that represents you well? The biggest concept we explored was designing content from the point of view of a user unfamiliar with your business and what it does.

₪ Promotional Strategies ₪

Press Releases – Sending out press releases can help your website ranking in search engines and can increase local visibility. Press releases are one of the best ways for potential customers to be reminded of your business without being hit with a sales pitch.

Videos – Engaging potential customers visually and in a way that is relatively high-tech can be very beneficial. The technology for video production can cost less than forty dollars and possibly nothing at all.

Articles – Similar to but distinct from press releases, articles go directly into search engine results and allow you to discuss topics that newspapers wouldn't necessarily run. These can serve to build your expertise in your area.

Photos – A great way to form a lasting impression in people's minds.

₪ Paid Advertising ₪

Sponsored Results – Paying for the "sponsored results" on the right side of search engine results is also a good idea. Advertising this way involves bidding on the best keywords

Banner Ads – Can be bought or traded with other sites. A relatively affordable option.

Facebook Ads – Give great customization, honing in with high accuracy on your intended audience.

₪ Search Engine Optimization ₪

This involves many carefully-crafted measures to ensure your web site and any materials you publish on the web have the best chance possible of ranking highest in search engine results. One key component of it is carefully attending to relevant keywords and their use in your web materials.

Conclusion

Ultimately, the Internet gives you far better results than most traditional advertising methods. And it's not going anywhere, it's just going to become more and more important to local businesses in upcoming years. If you aren't taking advantage of all the opportunities it offers, you have two choices - start taking advantage of them now, or fall behind when your competition does.

Where Should You Start?

We've covered quite a bit of ground so it's quite likely that you've got a bunch of ideas swimming around in your head, wondering where to start.

Our company specializes in helping local businesses get more customers by making them easy to find on the internet. If you'd like to learn how we can help you find new customers, as well as better engage the ones you already have, all at a much lower cost than most traditional methods of advertising, please get in touch with us.

You can email me directly at
Robert@LocalMarketingWeb.com

I would love to chat with you about how I can help your business attract more clients, and achieve a better web presence.

www.ingramcontent.com/pod-product-compliance
Lightning Source LLC
Chambersburg PA
CBHW071235170526
45165CB00003B/1112

* 9 7 8 1 4 6 3 7 0 4 1 5 5 *